DK READERS

Level 4

A Note to Parents

DK READERS is a compelling program for beginning readers, designed in conjunction with leading literacy experts.

Beautiful illustrations and superb full-color photographs combine with engaging, easy-to-read stories to offer a fresh approach to each subject in the series. Each DK READER is guaranteed to capture a child's interest while developing his or her reading skills, general knowledge, and love of reading.

The four levels of DK READERS are aimed at different reading abilities, enabling you to choose the books that are exactly right for your child:

Level 1 – Beginning to read
Level 2 – Beginning to read alone
Level 3 – Reading alone
Level 4 – Proficient readers

The "normal" age at which a child begins to read can be anywhere from three to eight years old, so these levels are only a general guideline.

No matter which level you select, you can be sure that you are helping your child learn to read, then read to learn!

LONDON, NEW YORK, MELBOURNE,
MUNICH, AND DELHI

Editor Kate Phelps
Designer Sooz Bellerby
Series Editor Alastair Dougall
Production Nicola Torode
Picture Researchers Bridget Tilly, Julia Harris-Voss

First American Edition, 2003
03 04 05 06 07 10 9 8 7 6 5 4 3 2 1
Published in the United States by DK Publishing, Inc.
375 Hudson Street, New York, New York 10014

Page design copyright © 2003 Dorling Kindersley Limited.

Published in Great Britain by Dorling Kindersley Limited.

Library of Congress Cataloging-in-Publication Data

Teitelbaum, Michael.
Batman's guide to crime and detection / Michael Teitelbaum.
p. cm. -- (DK readers)
Includes index.
Contents: The Dark Knight detective -- History of crime and the police
-- Today's police force -- Policing the streets -- Detectives --
Specialty teams -- The crime scene -- Forensics lab -- Fingerprints --
Footprints and other marks -- DNA matching -- Truth or lie? -- Vehicles
-- Weapons and equipment -- Computerization and communications --
Famous criminals -- Prisons.
ISBN 0-7894-9879-0 -- ISBN 0-7894-9755-7 (pbk.)
1. Detectives--Juvenile literature. 2. Criminal investigation--Juvenile
literature. [1. Batman (Comic strip) 2. Criminal investigation. 3.
Detectives.] I. Title. II. Series: Dorling Kindersley readers.
HV7922.T45 2003
363.25--dc21
                    2003004324

Color reproduction by Media Development and Printing Ltd, UK
Printed and bound in China by L Rex Printing Co., Ltd.

The publisher thanks the following for their kind permission to
reproduce their photographs: c=center; t=top; b=below; l=left; r=right
Corbis: 43br; **Bettmann** 14tl, 46tl, 47t; Anna Clopet 30b; Christel
Gerstenberg 7br; Ed Kashi 44b; Kent News and Picture/Sygma 39b;
Medford Historical Society Collection 9b; The Military Picture Library/
Eric Micheletti 16bl; Sygma /S.Costanza 14b; **Mary Evans Picture
Library:** 9tr; **Getty Images:** 37t; **HM Customs and Excise:** 15tr;
Popperfoto: 18tl; **David Roberts:** 43t; **Science Photo Library:** 24tl; BSIP,
Laurent 28b; Colin Cuthbert 21br; Adam Hart-Davis 40c; Peter Menzel
21tr; Hank Morgan 31tr; Sandia National Laboratories 25br; Andrew
Syred 20tl.

All other photographs © Dorling Kindersley.
For further imformation see: www.dkimages.com

The publisher thanks the following artists for their contributions to this
book: Quique Alcatena, Brian Apthorp, John Beatty, Brian Bolland,
Mark Buckingham, Robert Campanella, W. C. Carani, Mike Deodato,
Wayne Faucher, John Floyd, George Freeman, Drew Geraci, Tom
Grindberg, Tom Grummett, Scott Hanna, Edward Hannigan, James
Hodgkins, Jon Holdredge, Phil Jiminez, Jeff Johnson, Staz Johnson, Bob
Kane, Andy Lanning, Shawn Martinbrough, David Mazzucchelli, Scott
McDaniel, Jeff Moy, Graham Nolan, Tom Palmer, Howard Porter, Mark
Prudeaux, Darick Robertson, Anibal Rodriguez, Damion Scott, Lee
Weeks, Anthony Williams and Phil Winslade.

Discover more at
www.dk.com

Contents

JLA

BATMAN'S GUIDE TO

CRIME

AND DETECTION

Written by Michael Teitelbaum
Batman created by Bob Kane

The Dark Knight

I'm Batman. I've dedicated my life to fighting crime, stopping and catching criminals, and solving mysteries. I patrol Gotham City from its shadowy rooftops. I battle criminals and supervillains, using strength, skill, and cunning.

But some of the most difficult work I do is not so different from the work done by police officers and detectives in your city or town. Although much of what I do looks glamorous and exciting, I have caught just as many criminals using my knowledge of science, as I have using my fists.

Sometimes I act like a police officer, patrolling the streets. Sometimes my job is

Turning point
A terrible crime was the turning point in young Bruce Wayne's life. He saw his parents murdered, right before his eyes, shot dead by a gunman in a dark alley.

4

that of a detective. I've spent long hours working in my laboratory in the Batcave reviewing evidence, analyzing data, and examining the databases of known criminals.

In this book, you will learn about some of the techniques used by real police forces to investigate crimes. You'll also learn a bit about me and my world.

Detective-in-training
After his parents' murder, Bruce Wayne studied hard to learn all he could about fighting crime. He became an expert in the use of forensic science to catch criminals.

A history of crime

Harsh words
The word "Draconian," derived from the lawmaker Draco's name, has come to mean anything that is excessively harsh.

Physical training
In order to prepare himself to fight crime, Bruce Wayne went through rigorous physical training, including weight lifting, rock climbing, and gymnastics.

For as long as people have gathered in groups, crime has existed. Wherever human beings get together, laws are made to set a code of behavior for the tribe, the town, or the nation. The act of breaking those laws is called a crime, and the people who break the laws are called criminals.

One of the earliest systems of law and punishment for crimes was established in ancient Greece in 621 BC. There, a lawmaker named Draco drafted a code of behavior for people to follow. However, he came up with only one punishment for breaking the law. Whether you committed a serious crime like murder or robbery or were simply guilty of laziness, the sentence was the same—execution!

Almost a thousand years later, the Roman Emperor Justinian the Great established a fairer system of law. Different crimes received different punishments, according to the crime's gravity. Many of the modern world's legal systems are based on the Roman laws set forth by Justinian.

Combat ready
Bruce Wayne studied 127 styles of combat from boxing to karate.

But not all systems of law are based on the Roman model. In many tribal cultures in Africa and Asia, laws are made and justice is handed out by tribal chiefs, aided by holy men. In some tribes, shaman and witch doctors make the law.

The great lawmaker Justinian, as depicted in a Roman mosaic.

A history of the police

All societies have to deal with crime, and all have systems of law to establish what behavior is acceptable and what goes against the better common good. Those people given the task of preventing crimes and enforcing the law are called the police.

One of the first police forces was formed in Paris, France, in 1667. Chief of Police, La Reynie, took away a safe haven in the middle of the city, where criminals used to hide. He also started police foot patrols and police patrols on horseback called mounted police.

In 1750, crime had gotten so bad in London that a force of six men, known as the Bow Street Runners, was organized to patrol the streets and chase after criminals, night or day. The force soon expanded to fight the growing amount of crime.

Scary symbol
Bruce Wayne knew that the eerie look of the bat would strike fear into the hearts of criminals.

Peelers
London's Metropolitan Police became known as "bobbies" or "peelers" after Sir Robert Peel, the man who founded them.

As settlers in the United States moved westward during the 1800s, crime went with them. Bank robbers, train robbers, and cattle and horse thieves were a constant threat in the American old west. Local sheriffs and Federal Marshals were called out to enforce the law.

In 1850, a man named Allan Pinkerton founded a private detective agency in Chicago, which still exists today. Private detectives still help police in their investigation of crimes.

A London police officer from 1913.

The detective agency founded by Allan Pinkerton (seated left) had a logo with an eye in the center. It was the origin of the term "private eye," which is now applied to all private detectives.

Criminals beware! Batman made his first appearance in *Detective Comics* in 1939.

Today's police force

Modern police forces have many resources at their disposal. Patrol cars, plus other land, sea, and air vehicles, make searching for criminals or rushing to the scene of a crime fast and flexible. New communications systems, from walkie-talkies and radios to computers, allow for information to be shared quickly and easily.

Although foot and car patrols are the backbone of any police force, various specialty officers make up a modern police force. Highway patrol officers check for speeding vehicles. Specially trained diving units look for clues underwater. Mounted police still patrol on horseback, even in

A police officer from the New York Police Department.

Commissioner Gordon
James Gordon is Police Commissioner of Gotham City and one of Batman's greatest allies and friends.

some of the world's biggest cities like New York. They can move through gridlocked traffic more easily than police cars. Other officers are trained in crowd control.

Police stations are the command posts from which police forces do their work. A desk sergeant greets visitors and directs them to the proper department. Police stations contain offices, interrogation rooms, and a switchboard to receive emergency calls.

Regular police officers are assisted by support staff, traffic wardens, and even civilian volunteers. While some police officers are out on the street, others are doing the paperwork back at the station.

Gotham City's police officers wear their badge of office with pride.

Crime fighters
Led by Lt. Harvey Bullock (center), the Major Crimes Unit includes some of Gotham's finest detectives, including Renee Montoya (left) and Stan Kitch (right).

**Batman
on patrol**
Batman patrols
Gotham City at
night from the
rooftops and
shadows, using
surprise,
stealth, and
fear to fight
crime.

Policing the streets

Police officers patrolling the streets,
whether on foot or in police cars, are
the first line of defense in the war on
crime. Patrol officers work out of
station houses. Each station house is
responsible for a specific area of a
town or city. Police officers cover
these areas, known as their "beats,"
usually working in pairs.

When an emergency call comes
in, an operator contacts
the station house closest to
the crime. The dispatcher
at the station house then
radios the nearest police
patrol officers.

With their car's siren
blaring, the officers race to
the scene of the crime. Upon arrival,
the officers assess the situation.
If the crime is still in progress, or
weapons are being used or likely to
be used, or if a hostage has been

taken, the officers will radio to the police station for back-up. This is a request for additional officers to be sent to the crime scene.

If the crime is no longer in progress, officers check to see if anyone needs medical attention, in which case an ambulance is called. Victims and witnesses are interviewed, forms are filled out, and a report is written, which is filed back at the station. The officers who are first on the scene must also prevent the crime scene from being disturbed to preserve any evidence that might help catch a criminal.

The Bat-Signal
When a crime is committed in Gotham City requiring Batman's unique skills, the Bat-Signal is flashed against the night sky, letting the Dark Knight know that he is needed.

These New York cops are working together and patrol their beat by car. They are carrying radios for communicating with the station house and weapons to defend themselves against violent criminals.

British sleuth
The most famous fictional detective of all time (along with Batman) is Sherlock Holmes, created by British author Sir Arthur Conan Doyle in the 1890s.

Detectives

The job of investigating a crime, searching for clues and evidence, and identifying the perpetrator falls to the detectives. All large police forces have detective bureaus, a specialized division of the force. Most police detectives worked first as beat cops, then trained to become detectives.

When detectives arrive on the crime scene, they interview witnesses and victims. They also search the crime scene thoroughly, looking for evidence such as hair, clothing

The crime scene is sealed off by uniformed officers so that it is intact when the detectives arrive to investigate the crime.

fibers, fingerprints, blood for getting DNA samples, footprints, mud tracked in from outside, tire marks on a road or driveway, or marks made by tools to open a window, door, or safe.

By leaving the crime scene intact, detectives may try to recreate the sequence of events that led to the crime, to learn exactly what happened. Decoding this mystery, so that the correct person or persons can be apprehended for the crime is the main task of the detective.

Sometimes police dogs, also known as K-9 (shorthand for "canine") officers, assist detectives, using their highly developed sense of smell. If a vital clue like a piece of the suspect's clothing is found, the K-9 officers can match that smell when encountering the actual suspect.

Dogs are used by many police forces to sniff out evidence, especially illegal drugs. This dog is wearing a reflective harness for working at night.

Top detective Crispus Allen is a former beat cop who worked his way up to become a detective in the Gotham City Police Department.

Specialty teams

Special situations call for special police force teams. When skills beyond those of regular officers or detectives are needed, the police have many options.

The Bat-Suit
Batman's Bat-Suit is both fire and chemical resistant. Its Kevlar fibers (Kevlar is the material used in bulletproof vests) also serve as body armor.

When a big crowd gathers or a riot is feared, crowd-control officers are dispatched. They are equipped with helmets containing face shields, as well as body shields.

Sometimes criminals throw evidence, weapons, or even bodies into water, such as a lake, canal, or river, thinking that no one will be able to find them. Many police forces have special diving units. Trained divers, called frogmen, search for vital clues that may help to crack a case.

This S.W.A.T. officer from Los Angeles is wearing a fireproof suit and mask. His weapon is a high-powered shotgun.

Bomb squads are specially trained to respond to bomb threats. They must first determine if a real bomb is present. If it is, they then remove it from the area to a location where it can be safely disarmed or detonated.

In situations where police face heavily armed criminals, specially trained S.W.A.T. (Special Weapons and Tactics) teams can be called in. They wear armor, carry weapons, and are equipped to storm a building with the intention of capturing criminals and rescuing any hostages.

Police marksmen or sharp shooters are trained in the use of accurate high-powered rifles. They are used only as a last resort in siege and hostage situations.

JLA

Super police
The Justice League of America is a super-hero team that safeguards Earth.

Top team
The JLA are, clockwise from top right: Martian Manhunter, Green Lantern, Batman, Plastic Man, Aquaman, Wonder Woman, the Flash, and Superman.

Photographers make a record of the crime scene by taking pictures, which can be used as evidence.

Handy items
In addition to crime-fighting equipment, Batman's Utility Belt (below) contains many items useful at a crime-scene investigation, such as fingerprint powder, a camera, and a flashlight.

The crime scene

The area in which a crime takes place is called the crime scene. The police officers who arrive at the crime scene first have a few basic responsibilities. They assist any victims, determining whether medical attention is required. They detain any witnesses, making sure that they do not leave the crime scene so that detectives can interview them. They also seal off the crime scene, usually with police tape, protecting the area from being disturbed, making sure that potential evidence is not touched, and preventing unauthorized people from entering the crime scene.

Specialists arrive next. These include crime-scene investigators and photographers. The photographers thoroughly document the crime scene in photos, shooting the area from many angles. Sometimes the photographers use special lighting, such as ultraviolet and laser lights, to reveal clues that can't be seen under normal lighting.

night-vision lens

microphone

audio processor

Wearing protective clothes, crime-scene investigators collect evidence, such as fingerprints, blood, hair, fabric, and soil, in bottles and bags. They mark all evidence with a tag for easy identification.

Bat-tools
Batman's cowl contains equipment to help at a crime scene, including a night-vision lens, a microphone, and a listening device.

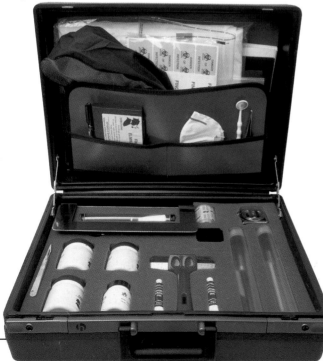

A crime-scene kit contains collecting bags and tubes; fingerprinting equipment; and an overall, cap, gloves, and shoe-covers to prevent the investigator from contaminating the crime scene.

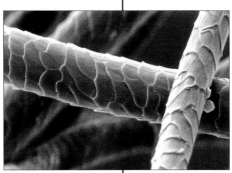

Great detail is revealed when fibers, hairs, or bullets are examined under the magnifying power of an electron microscope. This greatly enlarged image shows wool fibers.

The Batcave
Hidden beneath Wayne Manor, the multi-level Batcave serves as Batman's headquarters, sanctuary, and crime lab.

Forensics lab

The evidence gathered at a crime scene is taken to a forensics laboratory for analysis. Forensics is the science of crime and crime solving. These labs are filled with special equipment designed to analyze anything that might help solve a criminal case.

One of the forensic scientist's main methods of deduction is comparison. For example, the scientist will compare a hair taken from the crime scene with a hair from a suspect's head or compare a clothing fiber found in a suspect's car or home with a piece of

Batman's microscope
The Batcave is full of the very latest crime-fighting technology, including a super-powerful electron microscope.

clothing that was worn by the victim. Microscopic examination and chemical analysis are the two main methods of comparing evidence samples. A comparison microscope allows a scientist to view two samples side by side. This type of microscope was originally used to compare bullets and cartridge cases, but is now used to compare any small pieces of evidence.

Electron microscopes can magnify objects up to 150,000 times. This makes analysis and comparison extremely precise. Hairs, fibers, soil samples, and minerals can all be magnified to find a match.

An electron microscope is used to reveal the surface of specimens in incredible detail.

Ballistics is the study of guns and ammunition and is a very important part of forensic investigation. Guns fire cartridges, which are made up of bullets and cases. When a gun is fired, the cartridge moves through the gun barrel. As it travels at high speed, marks are made on the bullet. At the same time, the firing pin, which pushes the cartridge out of the gun, leaves a marking on the base of the cartridge case. Those marks can be compared to the marks on a test bullet fired from the same type of gun, to identify the weapon used during a crime.

Rogues Gallery
In the new Batcave, Batman has a computer platform on which he can display the files of Gotham City's many criminals.

The markings left on a bullet after it has been fired by a gun are unique to that particular weapon.

bullet

case

In Batman's world, his Batcave includes many elements of a real-life forensics lab. In addition to being the Dark Knight's headquarters in his ongoing war on crime, the Batcave contains a sophisticated electron microscope, a DNA spectrograph, and a full set of equipment dedicated to ballistics analysis.

The Batcave's central computer contains an enormous database with information about criminals Batman has encountered over the years. The Batcave also contains Batman's vehicles, costumes, trophies, and an amazing arsenal of crime-fighting equipment unique to the Dark Knight.

Centrifuge
By spinning liquids at high speeds, a centrifuge can separate out their component parts. This is another key element in the science of forensics.

North American brown bats live in the Batcave. Man-Bat felt right at home when he broke in, looking for the Dark Knight.

Fingerprints

No two alike
In 1858, British civil servant William Herschel discovered that no two people's fingerprints were exactly the same. He also observed that people's fingerprints did not change with age.

The use of fingerprints to identify criminals has been one of the great achievements in the history of fighting crime. Unlike hair color and style, eye color, or weight, a person's fingerprints cannot be changed. And no two sets of fingerprints are the same.

If fingerprints are left in a thick, wet substance, like blood, paint, or ink, then they are easy to see. Criminals, however, are not usually quite so accommodating. Most fingerprints are created by sweat or oils that are naturally present on anyone's fingers. These prints are called latent fingerprints.

The crime scene is dusted for fingerprints using aluminium powder and a special brush. Any prints are then lifted with special transparent tape. There are four main types of fingerprints: arch, loop, whorl and composite. Composite prints contain arches, loops and whorls.

Dusting brush

Aluminum dusting powder

Arch

Loop

Because latent fingerprints are not visible to the naked eye, special techniques are used to view them. Crime-scene investigators dust surfaces where prints are suspected to be located with a fine aluminum powder. The powder sticks to the oil and sweat revealing the print. The powder-covered print is then lifted using sticky transparent tape. Latent prints can also be revealed using special laser lights.

Law enforcement agencies keep records of the fingerprints of criminals so they have a huge database to check against when fingerprints are found at the scene of a crime.

Special glasses and a lamp enable this forensic scientist to see fingerprints as glowing marks.

Whorl   *Composite*

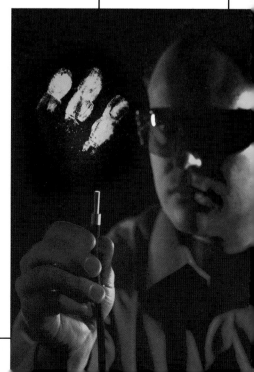

Criminal markings

Footprints or shoeprints are left at a crime scene in several ways. They can appear on a floor as a print made from mud, blood, paint, or oil. These are called visible or residue prints. They are photographed for comparison with the shoes of suspects. Shoes have recognizable patterns on their soles and also present distinctive signs of wear.

Footprints can also be found as impressions in mud or snow. These are called impression prints. They are photographed, then a hard cast is made of the print using a casting compound.

Like fingerprints, some footprints are latent, meaning that they are hard to see with the naked eye. Certain types of lighting and

A tire track

Flashy footprints
JLA member the Flash, the fastest man alive, uses positive grip treads on his boots for steady footing when he is tracking down criminals.

chemicals can reveal them.

Prints made by bare feet are similar to fingerprints. They have distinctive ridges just like hands and fingers. However, there is no database of these footprints in the police files.

Tire tracks also leave distinctive marks in mud and snow and wear out in recognizable patterns. They can be compared to the tires on the car of a suspect.

Tools such as hammers, chisels, knives, and wire cutters also leave patterns of ridges and nicks on doors, windows, and furniture at a crime scene. These marks can be matched to the tools' owner.

Super vision
Superman uses his telescopic vision to follow the footprints of an escaping criminal. He also has heat vision, super-hearing, and super-smell.

A muddy footprint. The sole of the shoe has left distinctive marks.

The Batcave's DNA spectrograph

DNA spectrograph
One of the many forensic tools in the Batcave, Batman's DNA spectrograph can quickly compare DNA patterns to see if they match.

DNA matching

When a British scientist named Alec Jeffreys discovered in 1984 how to create a profile, that is, a visual record of a human being's DNA, it was considered a major breakthrough in crime solving.

DNA (deoxyribonucleic acid) is the genetic code that makes up each human being. Within a single DNA molecule, there is a sequence of genetic information that is unique to each person. It's like your own personal barcode.

DNA profiles, which are sometimes called genetic fingerprints, can be obtained from a

Forensic scientists use computers to compare the genetic code of DNA found at a crime scene with that on file with the police. This computer screen shows part of a molecule of DNA.

person's body fluids (such as blood or saliva), skin, or hair. Any of these samples found at a crime scene can be profiled for DNA, then compared to the DNA profile of suspects, so that a positive identification can be made.

Although only a small sample of hair, skin, or body fluid is required to create a person's DNA pattern or profile, the sample must be kept free from contamination (dirt) that could ruin the results of the testing.

The accuracy of DNA matching makes it the best method yet for helping police to positively identify a person and to match his or her DNA with that of a sample found at a crime scene.

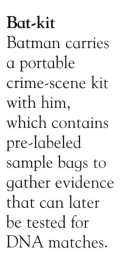

Bat-kit
Batman carries a portable crime-scene kit with him, which contains pre-labeled sample bags to gather evidence that can later be tested for DNA matches.

A model of part of a strand of DNA. It is shaped like a spiraling ladder. The "rungs" are pairs of chemicals called bases. The order of these bases makes up the genetic code.

Truth or lie?

A lie detector, also known as a polygraph, is a sensitive machine that measures several medical functions in a person's body—heart rate, blood pressure, respiratory rate (breathing), and electro-dermal rate (amount of sweat on a person's skin).

The theory behind the polygraph is that when a person tells a lie, his or her stress rate increases. When stress increases, heart rate, blood pressure, respiration, and sweating also increase.

Lasso of Truth
Wonder Woman's Lasso of Truth is the ultimate lie detector. Anyone caught in it must speak the truth.

When people take lie detector tests, the computer measures their response to questions about the crime of which they are accused.

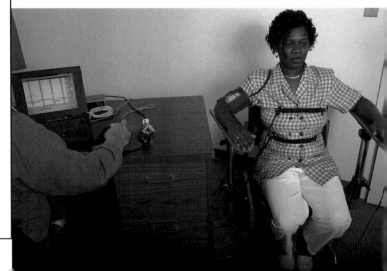

The polygraph is not a perfect method of determining the truth. In fact, some courts will not allow polygraph tests to be used as evidence.

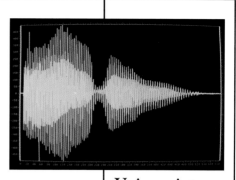

Voice prints
Police use voice prints, a visual record of a person's voice, to see if a suspect's voice matches that of a known criminal.

Brainwave analysis works in a slightly different manner. Words or pictures related to a crime are flashed on a computer screen, along with other words or pictures that have nothing to do with the crime. Electrical brain responses are measured through a headband equipped with sensors. When the brain recognizes an image or other information that it has seen before, a specific brain wave called a "mermer" occurs. Police can then determine whether or not the suspect has previously seen images related to the crime.

Mind reader
JLA member J'onn J'onzz, the Martian Manhunter, is a telepath and can read the thoughts of criminals and friends.

Police vehicles

The sound of a siren blaring and the sight of red flashing lights as a police car tears down the street alert pedestrians and motorists that the police are on the move.

Under their hoods, police cars are equipped with special motors that provide extra power during high-speed chases. Inside, they are packed with equipment. Two-way radios allow officers to communicate with other police cars and with their station house. Radar-detection units allow officers to measure the speed of passing cars.

Police cars are also equipped with laptop computers hooked up to wireless modems. This allows officers to receive all the information they need about a call—addresses,

Modern-day police officers still use horses in certain situations to patrol in parks and rocky terrain. They are also often used for crowd control.

Bomb threat! Special trucks used by the police bomb squad rush to the scene of bomb threats. There, specially trained officers disarm any explosives.

A police patrol car from Washington D.C.

suspects' names and criminal records, for example. It also helps them check on vehicles to see if they are stolen.

Batman also uses many vehicles in his battle against crime. The most famous of these is the sleek, speedy Batmobile. The Batmobile is bulletproof, and its bat-headed grille is strong enough to be used as a battering ram. It's got a 1,500 hp rocket-powered, fuel-injected engine to give the car a super burst of speed, and a parachute-assisted braking system. The Batmobile can turn right around in an instant by rising on a hydraulic lift, then spinning.

Batmobiles
Batman has had several Batmobiles, each an improvement on the last. The latest is the fastest and most high-tech one of all.

Bat-humvee
For off-road criminal pursuit, Batman uses the Bat-humvee. It has a raised suspension and special all-terrain tires.

Scooting along
Police from all over the world, including this police officer from Cuba, use fast-moving vehicles to catch criminals.

Two wheels
Batman's Batcycle has a bulletproof wind-guard and a superspeedy V-4 engine.

In addition to their cars, the police use many other vehicles. Motorcycles and bicycles enable officers to move more quickly through crowded city streets filled with traffic. Police boats patrol rivers around big cities, not only enforcing marine regulations, but also aiding police in land vehicles to keep fleeing criminals contained.

One of the most important vehicles available to the police is the helicopter. Its ability to fly at low altitudes and hover in one spot enables officers in the sky to coordinate with their partners on the ground. As police cars pursue a fleeing suspect in a car, a police helicopter can easily follow, radioing information to the officers below.

Batman also has a large collection of vehicles

at his disposal. Batcycles are often used by the Dark Knight's crime-fighting associates.

The Batplane is a state-of-the-art flying machine that includes a radar-shielded exterior, a breakaway canopy and a fully operational computer workstation.

Other airborne Bat-vehicles include the Bat-copter, based on a military attack helicopter, the Bat-glider and a collapsible, one-man Whirly-Bat, which the Dark Knight carries in the Batmobile's trunk.

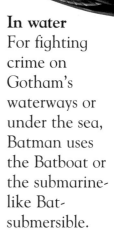

The Batboat

In water
For fighting crime on Gotham's waterways or under the sea, Batman uses the Batboat or the submarine-like Bat-submersible.

Batman's Whirly-Bat is a lightweight mini-copter.

A police boat patrols the water in Berlin, Germany.

Ultraviolet detector kit
Valuable goods can be marked with a substance that is invisible under normal light, but visible under ultraviolet light. If a thief steals the items, his or her hands reveal traces of the substance.

A New York police officer's nightstick.

Police equipment

The police have a large arsenal of tools at their disposal for fighting crime and protecting themselves. Guns are used only as a last resort for protection and defense. Officers in most countries carry a handgun in a holster. Police sharpshooters use high-powered rifles with special long-distance sights.

Police officers also carry nightsticks, which they use to subdue violent criminals. High-pressure water hoses are used to control big crowds. Spraying a strong stream of water at a rioting mob helps to keep it contained without injuring anyone. Tear gas is used to smoke criminals out of a building, allowing police to apprehend them.

A creative array of weapons and gadgets has always been part of Batman's crime-fighting arsenal.

Many stores, banks, and offices have closed-circuit cameras that record what people are doing inside and outside the building. Often, pictures are relayed to a control center, where the police or security guards keep a close watch on television monitors.

His famous Utility Belt, worn around his waist, contains many useful items, including a miniature camera, a set of lock-picking tools, teargas pellets, a laser torch, plastic-explosive grenades, a miniature cell phone, and a first-aid kit.

Unlike some real police, Batman doesn't use a gun. Then again, he doesn't need one. His chief weapon is the batarang, a bat-shaped throwing disk that is stored in his Utility Belt.

Batarangs
Batman has many types of Batarangs. They are made from steel alloys and are thrown like boomerangs.

37

Handcuffs

Phone taps
Police can
listen in on a
suspect's phone
calls using a
telephone tap.
Wires and a
transmitter are
connected to
the telephone
handset or to a
junction box
outside a
building.

tap

radio transmitter

For protection, the police wear
bulletproof vests, made from Kevlar,
a super-tough, yet flexible material.
They also wear helmets and carry
plastic shields when dealing with
crowd control or riots.

Handcuffs are an important tool.
Once a prisoner's hands are
restrained by the metal rings, the
officer has greater control over the
the suspect and the situation.

A magnifying glass, though
invented centuries ago, is still very
useful when searching for clues at a
crime scene. A telephoto lens comes
in handy when taking pictures of
a suspect from afar.

Among the many
gadgets at Batman's
disposal is the
grapnel, a powerful
grappling hook that
allows the Dark
Knight to climb up

the side of buildings or swing from rooftop to rooftop, high above the city. His multi-function binoculars provide conventional, infrared, and ultraviolet imaging and can bring an image of an object up to 60 times closer.

Batman's universal tool can be used to do many things. It contains screwdrivers, wrenches, electronic lock-picking devices, a drill, plus a recording and playback device.

The Rebreather is a miniature scuba device, five inches (12 cm) long, that provides Batman with breathable air underwater for up to two hours!

Fingerlight. Batman's fingerlight can provide narrow or wide beams of light in many colors of the spectrum, including infrared.

Police divers use special scuba gear to search for clues, vehicles, and even bodies underwater.

39

Communications

Often the difference between catching a criminal and losing one is the quality of communication between the first police officers at the scene of a crime, their back-up, officers at the station house, and specialists needed in extreme situations.

Keeping in touch
Batman has a communications device built into his cowl to help him monitor transmissions from hidden "bugs." He also has a GPS tracer in his boot so that his allies can track his whereabouts.

A British police officer using a walkie-talkie.

Two-way radios and walkie-talkies keep officers in touch with each other and with the station house. Computers can instantly send vital information to an officer at the crime scene. A car's license plate can be relayed to a central data base, and the officer can learn whether or not the car is stolen or belongs to a dangerous criminal.

Concealed cameras and hidden radio transmitters, called "bugs," help provide information to police. The transmitter, which can be hidden on a person or placed in an electrical outlet, relays an audio signal back to a receiver monitored by the police. A video camera hidden in a canvas camera bag can record images without anyone being aware that they are being taped.

Oracle
Wheelchair-bound Barbara Gordon, paralyzed by a bullet fired by the Joker, assumed the mantle of Oracle. She now sends information to Batman from her headquarters in Gotham's clocktower.

Famous criminals

Throughout history there have always been criminals who have captured the imagination of the public.

William H. Bonney, known to the world as Billy the Kid, was a gambler, a cattle and horse thief, and a ruthless killer. He was tracked down and killed in 1880 by a New Mexico sheriff named Pat Garrett.

In 1932, Clyde Barrow teamed with Bonnie Parker to form an infamous pair of robbers and murderers in the southwestern United States. They were featured in a 1967 film which added to their legend.

Butch Cassidy (Robert LeRoy Parker) and the Sundance Kid (Harry Longbaugh) led an outlaw gang of horse and

Catwoman
Petty thief turned cat burglar and master ninja, Catwoman is one of Gotham's trickiest rogues.

Two-Face
Former Gotham D.A. Harvey Dent's dark side emerged when a gangster spilled acid on half his face. The good and evil sides of his personality constantly battle for control.

A wanted poster for Bonnie and Clyde.

The Penguin
The Penguin is a criminal mastermind with an obsession for birds and trick umbrellas that contain all kinds of weapons.

Ned Kelly in his homemade suit of armor.

cattle rustlers and bank and train robbers in the American west of the 1890s. They too were immortalized and romanticized in a 1970 film that bore their names.

Ned Kelly was an Australian bank robber who lived in the 1800s. He and his gang lived in the bush, or outback, and survived a shootout with British soldiers. Kelly is famous for his amazing suit of armor, which he made himself out of iron. He was eventually captured and was hanged in 1880.

Arkham Asylum
Gotham City's most famous prison is Arkham Asylum for the Criminally Insane. This institution houses the worst of Batman's foes.

A prisoner behind the bars of his cell. Although prisoners are kept in their cells for long periods, they are allowed out for exercise, work, and recreation.

Prisons for criminals

When someone is convicted of a crime, that person usually goes to prison. The amount of time a person spends behind bars, known as their "sentence," depends on the severity of his or her crime.

Sometimes convicted criminals are sent to prison for rehabilitation, where they can be trained in skills that will allow them to be useful members of society upon their release. Some violent criminals are kept locked up in prison because they are dangerous and would be a public menace.

For many years, before jails were even thought of, criminals were punished by public humiliation, locked in stocks, which held their head and arms, or by more severe methods, such as execution, flogging, or torture. In Britain, criminals were sometimes sent to penal colonies in far off places like Australia or Tasmania.

Early forms of prisons for the poor have been around since the 1500s. The modern concept of prisons as places where criminals could be sent without being tortured or injured was developed by the Quakers of New Jersey and Pennsylvania in the late 1600s.

The design of a series of individual cells surrounding a central area was created in Philadelphia in 1790 and remains the blueprint for most prisons.

Specialized cells
Poison Ivy is kept behind thick Plexiglas in Arkham Asylum to keep her hypnotic pheromones within her cell.

Many of Gotham's worst criminals are kept behind bars in Arkham Asylum.

Dr. James Brussel, the famous criminal psychiatrist.

The Joker
Showing no remorse for his terrible crimes, the Joker takes pleasure in hurting those that Batman loves, unleashing psychological torture on the Dark Knight.

Forensic psychology

Psychology plays a role in the capture and rehabilitation of criminals. In the middle of the 20th century, American psychiatrist Dr. James Brussel, who was known as the "Sherlock Holmes of the couch," put forth the theory that, by studying the way a crime was carried out, it was possible to determine the type of person who might have committed it.

In 1957, he helped catch New York's "Mad Bomber," using his knowledge of criminal psychology to find a pattern in his crimes. In 1963, Dr. Brussel also helped capture Albert de Salvo, known as the "Boston Strangler."

Forensic psychologists are often asked to offer expert opinions in court cases, testifying as to whether a certain suspect's behavior

The "Mad Bomber," George Metesky (second right).

fits the crime of which he or she is accused. They will also be brought in to determine whether or not a suspect is insane and therefore unfit to stand trial.

With the help of these experts, police try to establish patterns of behavior to help them anticipate where a criminal may strike next, in hopes of preventing a crime from taking place.

Glossary

Analyze
To examine closely.

Apprehend
To capture and take into custody.

Arsenal
A collection of weapons.

Barcode
A symbol on a product that is read by a price-scanning machine.

Centrifuge
A machine that spins a liquid at high speed to separate its components.

Contaminate
Spoil evidence by polluting it with dirt.

Database
A place where information is stored.

Distinctive
Unusual and different.

Enforce
To make sure someone follows a law.

Forensics
The science of crime and criminals.

GPS tracer
A device for tracking someone's position. GPS stands for global positioning system.

Interrogation
The act of questioning someone closely.

Hostage
Someone held against their will.

Humiliation
Having your pride hurt.

Hydraulic
Operated by the pressure of fluid through pipes.

Illegal
Against the law.

Karate
A traditional Japanese form of combat.

Logo
A trademark.

Microscope
An instrument that produces a magnified image of an object.

Perpetrator
Someone who commits a criminal or anti-social act.

Pheromones
Chemicals secreted by some animals that affect the behavior of other animals.

Psychiatrist
Someone who studies the human mind.

Psychologist
Someone who studies human behavior.

Resistant
Protected against.

Restrain
To hold someone back.

Rigorous
Harsh or difficult.

Rustler
Someone who steals horses or cattle.

Spectrograph
A machine that analyzes light.

Stealth
Moving quietly.

Telephone tap
Equipment used to record phone calls.

Telephoto
A camera lens that produces a magnified image of an object.

Telescopic
An instrument that magnifies the image of an object.

Transmitter
A device that gives out radio waves.

Witness
Someone who sees a crime being committed.

Index